Simple Steps to *Salvation*
and Effective Prayer

Minister **Shenoa** T. Gibson

SIMPLE STEPS TO SALVATION AND EFFECTIVE PRAYER

Copyright © 2022 Minister Shenoa T. Gibson.

All rights reserved. No part of this book may be used or reproduced by any means, graphic, electronic, or mechanical, including photocopying, recording, taping or by any information storage retrieval system without the written permission of the author except in the case of brief quotations embodied in critical articles and reviews.

iUniverse books may be ordered through booksellers or by contacting:

iUniverse
1663 Liberty Drive
Bloomington, IN 47403
www.iuniverse.com
844-349-9409

Because of the dynamic nature of the Internet, any web addresses or links contained in this book may have changed since publication and may no longer be valid. The views expressed in this work are solely those of the author and do not necessarily reflect the views of the publisher, and the publisher hereby disclaims any responsibility for them.

Any people depicted in stock imagery provided by Getty Images are models, and such images are being used for illustrative purposes only.
Certain stock imagery © Getty Images.

Scripture quotations marked KJV are from the Holy Bible, King James Version (Authorized Version). First published in 1611. Quoted from the KJV Classic Reference Bible, Copyright © 1983 by The Zondervan Corporation.

Scripture quotations marked "AMP" are taken from the Amplified® Bible, Copyright © 1954, 1958, 1962, 1964, 1965, 1987 by The Lockman Foundation. Used by permission.

ISBN: 978-1-6632-1284-9 (sc)
ISBN: 978-1-6632-3993-8 (e)

Library of Congress Control Number: 2022909204

Print information available on the last page.

iUniverse rev. date: 05/16/2022

SALVATION SIMPLY PUT

ABSTRACT

Have you ever asked yourself what is "salvation" or how do I pray an effective prayer? Have you ever wanted to enjoy a life of abundance? Well, in this working guide, Dare Two Pray will lay out the pathway for you to take in a simplistic way to learn the basic principles and answer those questions. Let us get ready for our journey to obtaining salvation!

Minister Shenoa T. Gibson
Salvation Basics

Contents

Lesson 1: Introduction to Salvation and the Holy Ghost 1

Lesson 2: "What Is Prayer, Why Do We Pray, and How Do We Pray?" 7

Lesson 3: Positioning Yourself and Identifying God's Movement 13

Introduction 33

Objective 35

Lesson 1: Who is David? 37

Lesson 2: Definitions 39

Lesson 3: Psalm 23 – Encouragement 41

Lesson 4: Psalm 51 – Repentance 44

Lesson 5: Psalm 150 – Praise 47

About the Author 53

To my family. My mother, Evangelist Valerie Jackson: You have inspired me to be the best me I can be in Christ. You have been the rock of our entire family, and I appreciate your love and stern upbringing. I thank God for my sister. Jackie, you are a gifted and talented woman whom God has tremendously blessed. I thank the Lord for my younger brother Will and his wife Angela. I appreciate your continued support in all I do and being loved by you while we all grow in the grace and knowledge of Christ.

To my sons, DeJuan and Jalen Carter, you are my hearts, and I thank God for you. I strive to be the best mother I can be for you, and I keep you covered in prayer that God will allow you to flourish into the men that His will purposes for you. To my love, Daniel, thank you for being you. You are such a loving supporter of my gifts, talents, and call that God has entrusted me with. I thank God that He connected me with a person who allows me to be who God called and is calling me to be with no hesitation. God truly gave me a gift when He placed you and Nigel in my life.

To Jesus: as the song says, "I choose you again and again" and dedicate my life and this book to you. I pray that you will be pleased with the work I am doing for you. I pray that it will draw men and women to you now and for years to come if you delay your return.

Hello, I'm Minister Shenoa T. Gibson. I am writing this book being led by the Lord to share with you the concept that I found so essential and that I have shared with others to introduce them to salvation and cultivate an effective prayer life.

I would like to start out by asking you a couple of questions. If you say "yes" to any of them, this book is for you!

- Have you ever felt lost with no sense of direction?
- Have you ever encountered a situation in your life that you just knew you would never come through unscathed? You just knew that you would not make it.
- Have you made promises to God, yourself, and others just to gain some relief from pain, hurt, or even (dare I say) self-inflicted wounds? Have you ever thought to yourself, if I make it through this situation, I promise, I will do what I need to do to avoid this situation in the future?
- Have you ever wondered if you made a horrible mistake?
- Have you ever needed to be healed in your body and didn't see how it could happen?
- Have you ever looked toward heaven and said, "Lord, spare my child," "Lord, save my marriage," or "Lord, provide the funds for this bill"?

I have asked some of these questions and answered yes too! This book was written because I had to learn some important lessons in my life through various hardships. There were times when so many things happened in my life that I needed to find hope. I needed to get a prayer through. I needed relief. I turned my life over to Christ at eleven years old, strayed away in my teens, and rededicated my life in my early twenties and have never been the same since. My personal journey as a young wife, mother, divorcee, and now as a minister of the gospel who has found love again at the age of forty-three, coupled with reflecting over my life, has led me to this time where my heart is in pursuit of what God has for me.

Fulfilling the purpose for my life has become my focus. Being the founder of Dare Two Pray has opened my eyes to how effective prayer and obedience to God will transform your life. I find such joy in sharing the gospel! I love leading people back to Jesus or finding Him for the very first time it is so rewarding. As you complete this guide, know that no matter where you are in life, God can save, deliver, heal, and more!

When writing this guide, I wanted to share in a simple way what I find as basic concepts that will grow your faith and relationship with God.

Let Prayer Precede

Before we begin our lessons, let us pray. We want to precede all we do and preface each lesson with prayer. Please say the following together:

Dear Heavenly Father,

I pray for all of those who will read and complete this guide. I pray that you will open hearts and minds to receive what you have for them. Lord, you have abundant life for us. We gain an alliance in heavenly places, strategies to overcome obstacles, and eternal life. I pray that you will uncover your love for us, open closed eyes, soften hardened hearts, and grow us in Christian faith. I pray that your wisdom, understanding, and light will illuminate the path we choose when living life for you. I pray that this guide will enlighten the readers and be shared with those who need you or who want to teach others your ways. Lord, we pray against every barrier, blockade, and hindrance that will stop your people from accepting you as Savior, learning about the Holy Bible, and praying effective prayers to change situations and transform lives. We pray that this workbook will be seen all over the world. We come against confusion, fear, and doubt with all love and power that you gave us through the Holy Spirit. We thank you, Lord, for these blessings.

In Jesus's name, amen.

Welcome to the Dare Two Pray Work Guide. During our time together you will learn the basic principles of God's salvation plan, effective prayers, and living a life that the Bible refers to as "life more abundantly." Through the Holy Scriptures, assignments, and quizzes, you will research, uncover, and gain new spiritual revelation and insight about who God is, His powerful word, and how to apply it to your life. I have used this strategy and methods to show others that prayer works! When you apply these concepts to your life consistently, you will be amazed at how God will move in your life.

Lesson 1

Introduction to Salvation and the Holy Ghost

Salvation is an important part of those who believe in Jesus Christ and live their lives for the Lord. Why do we need to be "saved," you ask? From the beginning of time, when Adam and Eve sinned, life changed, and sin entered the world. God had to cover our sins then and sent His Son, Jesus, to pay the ultimate price of sin for us so we can have a chance to have eternal life. The Bible says, "Wherefore, as by one man sin entered into the world, and death by sin, and so death passed upon all men, for that all have sinned" (Romans 5:12). You may hear people say that being good, serving others, showing love, etc., is enough for us to go to heaven. I want to make it clear: nothing you can do will be enough to cover your own sins. Jesus cleansed us from our sins when He shed His blood on the cross for us, and we became redeemed. He paid the price for us. We need a Savior. We need salvation. We need Jesus!

Salvation – What does it mean to be saved? The definition of salvation, according to www.Merriam- Webster.com is "the act of saving someone from sin or evil." Being saved refers to accepting Jesus Christ as your Savior. This is a personal journey. Jesus died so your sins would be covered totally.

This sounds simple, doesn't it? Well, it is. Most often, people think about all the things they may have to give up, stop, turn away from, leave behind, etc. Approach salvation with simplicity and sincerity. Jesus wants to save you. Accept Him as your Savior today. Jesus loves you so much that He died for your sins. Isn't that worth submitting to Him? Would you die for someone? Think about it. You may say, yes, if it is my child or my parent. Most often the answer is no! We will negotiate for both lives to be saved. God gave His only Son to die for us. That is love! God has given us a chance to live, although sin has given us a sentence of death. Jesus was a perfect sacrifice for us. Jesus gave His life; it was not taken!

Read the scriptures below to see how the Bible explains being saved.

Romans 10:9–13 (in the Amplified version, AMP):

> Because if you acknowledge *and* confess with your mouth that Jesus is Lord [recognizing His power, authority, and majesty as God], and believe in your heart that God raised Him from the dead, you will be saved.
>
> For with the heart a person believes [in Christ as Savior] resulting in his justification [that is, being made righteous—being freed of the guilt of sin and made acceptable to God]; and with the mouth he acknowledges *and* confesses [his faith openly], resulting in *and* confirming [his] salvation.
>
> For the Scripture says, "WHOEVER BELIEVES IN HIM [whoever adheres to, trusts in, and relies on Him] WILL NOT BE DISAPPOINTED [in his expectations]." o for there is no distinction between Jew and Gentile; for the same *Lord* is Lord over all [of us], and [He is] abounding in riches (blessings) for all who call on Him [in faith and prayer].
>
> For "WHOEVER CALLS ON THE NAME OF THE LORD [in prayer] WILL BE SAVED.

Psalm 24:5: "He shall receive the blessing from the LORD, and righteousness from the God of his salvation."

John 3:16: "For God so loved the world, that he gave his only begotten Son, that whosoever believeth in him should not perish, but have everlasting life."

John 3:17: "For God sent not his Son into the world to condemn the world; but that the world through him might be saved."

If you have received salvation, document the date you received Jesus as your Lord and Savior.

_____/_____/_____ Congratulations! The angels in heaven and the Dare Two Pray family are rejoicing!!

Receiving the Baptism of the Holy Ghost

The Holy Ghost is such a precious gift. The names Holy Ghost and Holy Spirit are interchangeable. Many are afraid or think it is strange when they see someone speaking in tongues as the Spirit of God gives utterance. In this day and time, the Holy Ghost is presented or represented in such a manner as being a "play language," and dancing before God in the Spirit has become a commercial occurrence or form of entertainment. Funny memes used in social media posts have been a way of diminishing the real meaning and power of the encounter we have with God. While memes and expressive animations have their place, allow me to be clear and concise regarding this matter. The Holy Ghost is *real* and is God in Spirit. We serve a most powerful God, and His Spirit is not to be played with. The Holy Ghost is here to comfort, keep, lead, and guide you into all truth.

Receiving the baptism of the Holy Ghost requires repentance and complete surrender. Not of some parts of you, but *all* of you. The Bible says in Luke 6:46, "And why call ye me, Lord, Lord, and do not the things which I say?

God wants us to surrender our lives, pray to God to receive the gift of the Holy Ghost, and serve Him in our daily lives by following His commandments. Praying to receive the Holy Spirit means asking the Lord to fill you with the Holy Ghost. Imagine you need some water. It is hot and you need relief. Someone gives you a bottle of water and sits it next to you. Is this helping you? Can you feel the relief from looking at the bottle of cold water? No, you need to do more. There is a difference between having a bottle of water and quenching your thirst by drinking the water. You now open the bottle and empty the contents of the bottle into your body. You feel the coolness of the water as it flows from your mouth to your stomach. It provides a relief from being dry and parched. This is an analogy of receiving the Holy Ghost. The Spirit of God is here, but is He inside you? Ask God to fill you with His Spirit. You will feel the presence of God on the inside of you. Renewal is happening. The Bible says in Psalm 42:1, "As the hart (type of deer) panteth after the water brooks, so panteth my soul after thee, O God."

The scriptures that follow are to uncover the biblical verses pertaining to the Holy Ghost:

Acts 2:1–4:

> And when the day of Pentecost was fully come, they were all with one accord in one place.
>
> And suddenly there came a sound from heaven as of a rushing mighty wind, and it filled all the house where they were sitting.
>
> And there appeared unto them cloven tongues like as of fire, and it sat upon each of them.
>
> And they were all filled with the Holy Ghost, and began to speak with other tongues, as the Spirit gave them utterance.

Acts 2:38: "Then Peter said unto them, Repent, and be baptized every one of you in the name of Jesus Christ for the remission of sins, and ye shall receive the gift of the Holy Ghost."

Acts 19:2–3: "He said unto them, have ye received the Holy Ghost since ye believed? And they said unto him, we have not so much as heard whether there be any Holy Ghost. And he said unto them, unto what then were ye baptized? And they said, Unto John's baptism."

John 14:26: "But the Comforter, which is the Holy Ghost, whom the Father will send in my name, he shall teach you all things, and bring all things to your remembrance, whatsoever I have said unto you."

Luke 3:16: "John answered, saying unto them all, I indeed baptize you with water; but one mightier than I cometh, the latchet of whose shoes I am not worthy to unloose: he shall baptize you with the Holy Ghost and with fire."

Matthew 28:18–20:

> And Jesus came and spake unto them, saying, all power is given unto me in heaven and in earth.
>
> Go ye therefore, and teach all nations, baptizing them in the name of the Father, and of the Son, and of the Holy Ghost:
>
> Teaching them to observe all things whatsoever I have commanded you: and, lo, I am with you always, even unto the end of the world. Amen.

The Holy Ghost is a gift. Yes, I needed to repeat it. Everyone can receive the Holy Ghost. A question that is posed frequently is "What does the Holy Ghost feel like?" It is not a "spooky" event, as I have heard some say. People have said that they felt the Spirit of God come upon them, and they got scared and stopped praying. The feeling is not like any other. People react differently when they feel the presence of the Lord because is unfamiliar to them. People may feel an overwhelming need to cry; some may shout, some may run, and some may jump or dance. Being moved by the power of God is an amazing feeling. It is total submission to God. You receive *power* when you are filled with the Spirit (Acts 1:8)! I think everyone appreciates having power!

The evidence of being filled with the Holy Ghost is speaking in tongues. Let's not get confused with the concept of "feeling" the Spirit of God and being "filled" with the Spirit of God. The presence of God can be felt undeniably. Jesus came on the scene and changed the entire way of how we access God and the power we carry within us daily. We have a direct connection now. No longer do we need priests to go to God for us. We, through Christ have been given divine access to Him and through grace we are saved through faith. The Holy Ghost will keep us.

Are you wondering how complicated it is to accept Jesus as your personal Savior?

Here are the steps to getting saved and filled with the Holy Spirit:

Pray. Talk to the Lord and express your intent to give your life to Him.

Believe in Jesus Christ. Believe He is the Son of God. Believe that He died on the cross for your sins. Believe that He rose from the dead on the third day with all power.

Repent by asking God for forgiveness of your sins, and commit to living a life pleasing to the Lord.

Confess with your mouth that Jesus is Lord.
Accept him in your heart.
Ask for the Holy Spirit.
Live your life for the Lord.

I know, the steps seems so simple. Yes, when someone yields themselves unto the Lord with a sincere heart it is just that simple. What is stopping you today? Doesn't this sound amazing? There is so much we are missing outside of the Lord's arms. Our loving God wants everyone to accept him as Savior and Lord of their lives and receive the gift of the Holy Ghost and fire.

Lesson 2

"What Is Prayer, Why Do We Pray, and How Do We Pray?"

In this lesson, we will discuss prayer and why it is needed. In the beginning of the workbook, I asked you questions to ponder. I reflected on my life and all the circumstances that caused me to go to God in prayer. The reason I was able to get through my hardships was prayer. I recall a time when I had a nervous breakdown—yes, a saint of God had a nervous breakdown. How did I overcome? Prayer! When prayer goes forth on behalf of others, and when you pray about your circumstances, those prayers will have effects. When you fervently pray to Jesus, He will hear and answer you. As you read this lesson, think about your life. Is there anything that you need to pray about?

What Is Prayer?

Definition of Prayer: A devout petition to God or an object of worship. A spiritual communion with God or an object of worship, as in supplication, thanksgiving, adoration, or confession.

Why Do We Pray?

Communication with God is important to do daily. Jesus commanded us to pray and not to grow weary doing so. Praying allows us direct access to God and His will and plan for our lives. Prayer provides directions during decision making, we pray one for another (intercede), and lastly, we pray to give honor to the Most High God.

These are just a few reasons we pray. Prayer must become a daily part of life while on this Christian journey. Once you pray daily, your life will never be the same. See the scripture references below.

1 Thessalonians 5:17–19, 25: "Pray without ceasing. In everything give thanks: for this is the will of God in Christ Jesus concerning you. Quench not the Spirit …. Brethren, pray for us."

Luke 18:1: "And he spake a parable unto them to this end, that men ought always to pray, and not to faint."

How We Pray

The blueprint for prayer has been left for us to refer to in God's word. This lays out the breakdown of our prayers which will be mentioned in the "Constructing a Prayer" section of the lesson.

"The Lord's Prayer" – Read Matthew 6:9–13

> After this manner therefore pray ye: <u>Our Father</u> which art in heaven, hallowed be thy name.
>
> Thy kingdom come, thy will be done in earth, as it is in heaven.
>
> Give us this day our daily bread.
>
> And forgive us our debts, as we forgive our debtors.
>
> And lead us not into temptation but deliver us from evil: For thine is the kingdom, and the power, and the glory, forever. Amen.

Constructing an effective prayer – The components of prayer:

Who you pray to – Lord, God, Father, etc. – His will be done in our lives.
Who you pray for – Us, mom, sister, etc.
Pray against whom/what – evil, barriers, unseen blockades, demonic forces, etc.

Show gratitude/worship/admiration to God – for advance blessings, blessings already received, just because He deserves it.

Amen – it is complete/finished.

In the beginning when incorporating these components, it may feel a bit like you have to think about it. It will become the norm as you incorporate praying into your daily life.

Research Activity /Discussion- How to Pray Regarding Specific Challenges

List some things that hold you back from praying and spending time with God:

1.

2.

3.

What areas of your life, what emotional or physical challenges, do you need prayer for (name two or three)?

Using the Bible, find scriptures in relation to the areas you listed that you find encouraging.

1.

2.

3.

Homework: Developing Your Effective Prayer

Choose one of the challenges you listed and an encouraging scripture; then create a prayer that addresses the challenge using the components of prayer. Be ready to share.

Homework Completion Check Point

Lesson 1 & 2 Quiz: Using the scripture references and discussion, answer the questions below.

What do we believe? _____
Define prayer: _____
Why seek salvation? _____
How do you seek salvation?
_____
_____

What is another name for the Holy Ghost? _____
What day did the Holy Ghost come? _____
What sound was made in the house, and where did it come from?
_____

What does "one accord" mean? _____
What else will you receive when you receive the Holy Ghost?
_____

What are the components of prayer?
_____   _____   _____
_____   _____

What is the name of the "blueprint" left for us? Where is it found?
_____

How often should you pray? _____

Homework Assignment

Pray for 10–15 minutes, using the prayer you created in the "Addressing Challenges in Prayer" activity. Memorize the Prayer in Matthew chapter 6.

Homework completion check: Recite the Lord's Prayer- Matthew 6:9–13

Lesson 3

Positioning Yourself and Identifying God's Movement

In this lesson, you will learn how to position yourself to hear from God and identify the move of God. It is truly rewarding being able to see the move of God in our lives. At times, we know it can be a challenge focusing or even identifying the move of God. Let us talk about how to gain access and be successful in hearing from the Lord.

Common Questions: Have you ever asked these questions?

Why can't I hear from God?
How can I hear from God?
Is God moving in my life?

Why can't I hear from God? Simply put, you are not in fellowship with God.

The Bible says in John 8:47, "Whosoever is of God and belongs to Him hears (the truth of) God's words; for this reason, you do not hear them: because you are not of God and you are not in fellowship with Him."

Romans 3:23 says, "For all have sinned and come short of the glory of God"

This is the reason people outside of fellowship cannot hear from God. Ask God, "What must I do to be saved, to hear from you, to get into your presence?"

How can I hear from God? Simply put, repent, and turn to God.

Second Chronicles 7:14 says: "If my people, which are called by my name, shall humble themselves, and pray, and seek my face, and turn from their wicked ways; then will I hear from heaven, and will forgive their sin, and will heal their land."

When you accept God in your life and decide to live for Jesus, you become a new creature. Second Corinthians 5:17 says, "Therefore if any man be in Christ, he is a new creature: old things are passed away; behold, all things are become new." You have now been reconciled with Christ.

Is God moving in my life? Simply put, *yes*! Every day!

Psalm 86:7 says, "In the day of my trouble I will call upon thee: for thou wilt answer me."

Psalm 91:5 says, "He shall call upon me, and I will answer him: I will be I with him in trouble; I will deliver him and honor him."

Isaiah 65:24 says, "And it shall come to pass, that before they call, I will answer; and while they are yet speaking, I will hear."

Did you know God is already here and listening to you? He wants to assure you that when your heart is overwhelmed, and you run to Him, He will answer you! He will move in your life. He will meet your need, save your soul, remove you from the path of destruction, and honor your requests.

As believers of Christ, we expect healing, we expect prayers to be answered, and we expect a move of God. At times, we are focused more on the negative in life rather than the blessings that God gives us daily. We talked about the reasons that your prayers are not answered, and that it is important to be able to see that hand of God move in your life.

In this next lesson, we will acknowledge the move of God in our lives by creating a "Move of God" journal.

7-Day "Move of God" Journal Activity

The purpose of this journal is to capture when you identify a "move of God" after you have prayed. God is always answering prayers and denying prayers to protect us, guide us, or even provoke us to reevaluate our actions, thoughts, and deeds. We may even need to check our heart's intentions. Practicing prayer and identifying God's move will create a deeper relationship with the Lord. It will transform us from practice to living a committed life for Christ.

Directions:

Using the Move of God Journal pages provided, write down heartfelt prayers daily (one to three prayers)

Use the Components of Prayer to create the effective prayer.

You may use the items from Lesson 2 and scriptures to add substance to your prayer. You may record a new prayer and research new scriptures of your choice.

- Note: Scriptures are not needed for each of these prayers—the Components of Prayer are required

Each day, take time to be in quiet space to identify if God has answered of those prayers

Record what has been realized during your moments with God

Thank God for all His blessings that He has already granted you daily. See this scripture if you need a hint as to why you should thank God. "It is of the Lord's mercies that we are not consumed, because his compassions fail not. They are new every morning: great is thy faithfulness" (Lamentations 3:22–23).

This activity will take you about 15–45 minutes. Journal entries are to be completed daily. Consistency is key. As you spend more time with God and reading His word, you will see your life change. Your purpose for doing this will change. You will find yourself with an increased desire to read, write, and pray more as you continue to do this activity.

Maintain Your Focus

Matthew 26:41 says, "Watch and pray, that ye enter not into temptation: the spirit indeed is willing, but the flesh is weak." If your mind wanders, take a minute to acknowledge the thought and refocus on your task. Things will get easier the more you commit this time with the Lord. Your hunger and thirst will increase for the things of the Lord.

During this time, do not be discouraged if a prayer that you have recorded is not answered within this time frame.

God's timing is not our timing. If an answer has not been realized or manifested, it does not mean that God did not hear or will not answer. Remember to continue to repeat the prayer, believe God, and pray against any form of hindrance. God's will is going to supersede our fleshly wants also. This means if the prayer you are praying is centered on selfishness or things that are contrary to God's plan and word, the delay will give you a chance to course correct your prayer to align with God and the purpose He has for you.

Listen, if you are compelled to cry, *cry!* If you are compelled to scream, *scream!* If you are compelled to be silent, *be silent!* If you are compelled to shout and dance before the Lord, *dance and shout!* If you are speaking in tongues as the Spirit of God gives utterance, *speak*, and build up your most holy faith! This is your intimate time with God, and you want to feel the presence of God while spending time with Him. So—surrender, and let God move!

Additional Scripture Readings

> In the same way the Spirit [comes to us and] helps us in our weakness. We do not know what prayer to offer *or* how to offer it as we should, but the Spirit Himself [knows our need and at the right time] intercedes on our behalf with sighs *and* groanings too deep for words.

And He who searches the hearts knows what the mind of the Spirit is, because the Spirit intercedes [before God] on behalf of God's people in accordance with God's will.

And we know [with great confidence] that God [who is deeply concerned about us] causes all things to work together [as a plan] for good for those who love God, to those who are called according to His plan *and* purpose. (Romans 8:26–28 AMP)

Lesson 3 Knowledge Check

Name the 3 common questions that one asks regarding God.
_____

_____ _____

What can you do to hear from God? _____

What does Romans 3:23 say? Why is this important to know? -
_____
_____
_____

True or False: Evil is present, and my flesh is strong to overcome temptation. _____

When praying and spending time with God, what is important to remember?
_____
_____

How often do you pray? _____

Discussion

Submit a praise report to share in class or reflect on. A praise report is a realized or manifested answer, intervention, or blessing received from a prayer you prayed.

_____
_____
_____
_____
_____
_____
_____
_____
_____
_____
_____

Congratulations!

At this time, you have completed the basic lessons of what we believe the plan of salvation, and effective prayers.

Continuing to implement these teachings, I believe that your life will be fulfilled, and you will experience the abundance of God's love and provision for you. You will also develop a closer relationship with God the Father and His presence will be revealed to you more and more.

This Christian journey is a lifetime commitment.

Take this oath

I will commit to prayer and seeking God for answers and direction.
I will commit to serving God, our families, and our communities.

There is a reward at the end! Hearing God say, "Well done, my good and faithful servant," is our goal as we enter into the kingdom of heaven.
I hope you have enjoyed this lesson with *Dare Two Pray*. God bless you!

If you need a prayer partner, reach out to Dare Two Pray:
24/7 email for prayer requests: DareTwoPray@gmail.com
Follow us on Instagram for daily inspiration: @Daretwopray
Arise In Power Hour
Dare Two Pray Intercessory Prayer Line:
To join us, dial 1-800-309-2350 access code 1880784.

Minister Shenoa T. Gibson

Move of God Journal

Day 1

Move of God Journal

Day 2

Minister Shenoa T. Gibson

Move of God Journal

Day 3

Move of God Journal

Day 4

Minister Shenoa T. Gibson

Move of God Journal

Day 5

Move of God Journal

Day 6

Minister Shenoa T. Gibson

Move of God Journal

Day 7

Answer Key

Homework Completion Check Point

Lesson 1 & 2 Quiz

Using the scripture references and discussion, answer the questions below.

What do we believe? We believe in the Trinity—Father God, Jesus Son of God (God in Flesh), Holy Ghost (God in Spirit) – 3-in-1

Define Prayer: A devout petition to God or an object of worship. A spiritual communion with God or an object of worship, as in supplication, thanksgiving, adoration, or confession.

Why seek salvation? _____Personal answer_____

How do you seek salvation?

God wants us to surrender our lives, pray to God to receive the gift of the Holy Ghost, and serve Him in our daily lives by following His commandments.

What is another name for the Holy Ghost? _____Comforter_____

What day did the Holy Ghost come? _____Pentecost_____

What sound was made in the house and where did it come from?_____ mighty___rushing wind_____

What does "one accord" mean? _____two or more people doing something at the same time_____

What else will you receive when you receive the Holy Ghost? _____ Fire_____

What are the components of prayer?

Who you pray to – Lord, God, Father, etc. – His will be done in our lives.

Who you pray for – Us, mom, sister, etc.

Pray against whom/what – evil, barriers, unseen blockades, demonic forces, etc.

Show gratitude/worship/admiration to God – for advance blessings, blessings already received, just because He deserves it.

Amen – it is complete/finished.

What is the name of the "blueprint" left for us? Where is it found? ____ The Lord's Prayer Matthew 6:9–13__

How often should you pray? _____without ceasing_____

Lesson 3 Quiz

Name the 3 common questions that one asks regarding God.
Why can't I hear from God?
How can I hear from God?
Is God moving in my life?
What can you do to hear from God? Simply put, repent and turn to God.

"If my people, which are called by my name, shall humble themselves, and pray, and seek my face, and turn from their wicked ways; then will I hear from heaven, and will forgive their sin, and will heal their land" 2 Chronicles 7:14).

What does Romans 3:23 say? Why is this important to know?

_____For all have sinned and come short of the glory of God_____
_____
_____

True or False: Evil is present, and my flesh is strong to overcome temptation. _____

When praying and spending time with God, what is important to remember?

_____Consistency is key—don't get discouraged; other answers may be acceptable_____
_____

How often do you pray? ____without ceasing (not a duplicate/important) _____

Minister Shenoa T. Gibson

**Welcome
To
Dare Two Pray
Bible Study**

Introduction

Dare Two Pray was designed to for fellowship and encouraging one another, building one another up in love, and praying together to reap the benefits that God has for us.

We believe what the Bible says in St. Matthew 18:20, "For where two or three are gathered together in my name, there am I in the midst of them."

This Bible study can be used in groups, coaching sessions, pairs, or as an individual study. We will introduce you the book of Psalms in the Holy Bible. In this life we sometimes look at ourselves as unworthy of God's blessings because of sin, we may need to be encouraged and find hope, we may need to learn to praise God through our circumstances. I am excited to share that David, whom you may know or will meet during this lesson, will help us explore these things through a few of his writings! You may also relate to his life and uncover some helpful and meaningful insight from David's ideals. Psalms is made up of 150 chapters; we have selected three prominent ones to focus on for this study. Before we proceed, let us pray:

Today's Prayer

Dear Heavenly Father,

As we begin this session, allow us to be in one accord with open hearts and minds. Open our understanding, and give us revelation in your word. Help us hear what you are saying to us through your word, that we may hide it in our hearts, that we may not sin against you. We pray against anything that will hinder the learning and delivery of your word. We give you this time and pray you honor it, that it may yield fruit and cause us to grow in the grace and knowledge of you. We thank you for all you have done for us and all you will do for us. In Jesus's name, we pray. Amen!

Objective

The objective of this study is to read and discuss the scriptures found in the book of Psalms in the Holy Bible. This is a book that has so much depth and meaning, and we will touch on some a few key chapters that I believe will have an impact in your life. You will find that the scriptures and concepts are easy to apply in your life. We will define commonly used terms to impart and increase your understanding and knowledge of this book of the Bible.

Our focus during the lessons will highlight the following:

- Who is David?
- Define Psalm, Praise, and Worship
- Psalm 23 – Encouragement
- Psalm 51 – Repentance
- Psalm 150 – Praise
- Knowledge Check

Lesson 1

Who is David?

In this lesson we will list facts about David. David was a very notable person in the Bible. His life had many ups and downs, trials and tribulations, deceit and despair, but also songs and prayers. As you read this lesson, keep in mind this man, David, and see if there are any parallels between your life and his.

- David was the youngest son of Jesse.
- David was a young shepherd.
- David was a musician.
- David loved God.
- David was filled with the Holy Ghost.
- David was small in stature and unassuming and had great strength and courage.
- David defeated a lion, a bear, and a giant named Goliath with a slingshot and stones.
- David was anointed king of Israel (God's chosen people) and built an empire.
- David feared and reverenced God.
- David committed adultery with a married woman and impregnated her.
- David tried to cover up his actions and ordered a murder.
- David was a spouse and parent.
- David displeased God.
- David suffered consequences of sin.
- David repented and turned from his ways of sin back to God.
- David experienced the death of a child.
- David's son turned against him.
- David escaped death by leaving his country during a revolt.

- David returned to Israel.
- David was said to be a humble man and obedient, "a man after God's own heart."
- David wrote about 75 Psalms of the 150 in the book of Psalms.
- David anointed his son Solomon to be his heir.
- David sought God throughout his life even if he got off track.
- David calmly died.

Why do you think knowing about David's life is important?

What are some of the parallels in David's life that you can relate to in your life?

_____
_____
_____
_____

Lesson 2

Definitions

Learning frequently used terminology is important as we move forward in the lesson. Whether you have used and heard these terms before or are just learning them now, let the meaning and use of the words seep into your heart. Using your resources, define the terms below and be ready to discuss or write down your thoughts.

What are psalms?

What is praise?
_____

What is worship?
_____

Provide the definition for the following words:

Sanctuary
Firmament
Bloodguiltiness
Contrite
Repentance
Timbrel
Psaltery

Minister Shenoa T. Gibson

Hyssop
Transgression
Righteousness

What does defining these terms help us understand?
_____

When you think of these terms, they create an atmosphere. They usher in the presence of God. When God is present, we have access to miracles.

Lesson 3

Psalm 23 – Encouragement

In this section, we will review a few key psalms in the Bible. These psalms have distinctive meanings. As you read these chapters and verses, be ready to discuss how you relate to them and the meaning you take from these scriptures. In this lesson, we will read Psalm 23 and discuss the meaning of each verse together or write down your take-a-way from the reading.

Psalm 23, King James Version (KJV)

> The LORD IS MY SHEPHERD; I SHALL NOT WANT.
> He maketh me to lie down in green pastures: he leadeth me beside the still waters.
> He restoreth my soul: he leadeth me in the paths of righteousness for his name's sake.
> Yea, though I walk through the valley of the shadow of death, I will fear no evil: for thou art with me; thy rod and thy staff they comfort me.
> Thou preparest a table before me in the presence of mine enemies: thou anointest my head with oil; my cup runneth over.
> Surely goodness and mercy shall follow me all the days of my life: and I will dwell in the house of the Lord forever.

Psalm 23, Amplified Bible

> The Lord is my Shepherd [to feed, to guide and to shield me],
>   I shall not want.
> He lets me lie down in green pastures;
>   He leads me beside the still *and* quiet waters.
> He refreshes *and* restores my soul (life);

He leads me in the paths of righteousness
for His name's sake.
Even though I walk through the [sunless] valley of the shadow of death,
I fear no evil, for You are with me;
Your rod [to protect] and Your staff [to guide], they comfort *and* console me.
You prepare a table before me in the presence of my enemies.
You have anointed *and* refreshed my head with oil;
My cup overflows.
Surely goodness and mercy *and* unfailing love shall follow me all the days of my life,
And I shall dwell forever [throughout all my days] in the house *and* in the presence of the Lord.

Notes Page

Notes Page

Lesson 4

Psalm 51 – Repentance

This psalm is centered around repentance. The reminds us that we all have sinned and fall short. It is not the sin; it is what we do after the sin is committed. Do we continue in the way of sin or do we turn away from sin and become deeply sorry to God for the thoughts, words, or deeds that did not please God? Take a look at what David did after the prophet Nathan told David about the consequences of sin.

Psalm 51 is a contrite sinner's prayer for pardon. Here it is in the Amplified version:

> To the Chief Musician. A Psalm of David; when Nathan the prophet came to him after he had sinned with Bathsheba.
> Have mercy on me, O God, according to Your lovingkindness;
> > According to the greatness of Your compassion blot out my transgressions.
>
> Wash me thoroughly from my wickedness *and* guilt
> > And cleanse me from my sin.
>
> For I am conscious of my transgressions *and* I acknowledge them;
> > My sin is always before me.
>
> Against You, You only, have I sinned
> > And done that which is evil in Your sight,
> > So that You are justified when You speak [Your sentence]
> > And faultless in Your judgment.
>
> I was brought forth in [a state of] wickedness;
> > In sin my mother conceived me [and from my beginning I, too, was sinful].
>
> Behold, You desire truth in the innermost being,

And in the hidden part [of my heart] You will make me know wisdom.
Purify me with hyssop, and I will be clean;
    Wash me, and I will be whiter than snow.
Make me hear joy and gladness *and* be satisfied;
    Let the bones which You have broken rejoice.
Hide Your face from my sins
    And blot out all my iniquities.
Create in me a clean heart, O God,
    And renew a right *and* steadfast spirit within me.
Do not cast me away from Your presence
    And do not take Your Holy Spirit from me.
Restore to me the joy of Your salvation
    And sustain me with a willing spirit.
Then I will teach transgressors Your ways,
    And sinners shall be converted *and* return to You.
Rescue me from bloodguiltiness, O God, the God of my salvation;
    Then my tongue will sing joyfully of Your righteousness *and* Your justice.
O Lord, open my lips,
    That my mouth may declare Your praise.
For You do not delight in sacrifice, or else I would give it;
    You are not pleased with burnt offering.
My [only] sacrifice [acceptable] to God is a broken spirit;
    A broken and contrite heart [broken with sorrow for sin, thoroughly penitent], such, O God, You will not despise.
By Your favor do good to Zion;
    May You rebuild the walls of Jerusalem.
Then will You delight in the sacrifices of righteousness,
    In burnt offering and whole burnt offering;
    Then young bulls will be offered on Your altar.

Notes:

Lesson 5

Psalm 150 – Praise

In this lesson we will read Psalm 150 (KJV) and discuss the meaning of each verse together.

> Praise ye the Lord. Praise God in his sanctuary: praise him in the firmament of his power.
> Praise him for his mighty acts: praise him according to his excellent greatness.
> Praise him with the sound of the trumpet: praise him with the psaltery and harp.
> Praise him with the timbrel and dance: praise him with stringed instruments and organs.
> Praise him upon the loud cymbals: praise him upon the high sounding cymbals.
> Let everything that hath breath praise the Lord. Praise ye the Lord.

Notes Page

_____
_____
_____
_____
_____
_____
_____

These lessons were designed to show you parallels to your life, define key terms in the Bible, and discuss scriptures and meanings. Now let's test your knowledge. You will take a short quiz to see what you retained during the lesson.

Bible Study Knowledge Check

1. Who is the writer of the Book of Psalms? _____
2. Circle True or False: David wrote 75 of the 150 chapters of Psalms.
3. Fill in the blanks: The Lord is my _____ I shall _____. Where is it found? _____
4. What is the name of the valley referred to in Psalm 23? _____
5. What is my head anointed with? _____
6. How many instruments are used to praise God? _____
7. Where do you praise God? _____
8. Circle True or False: David was the oldest son of Jesse.
9. Define Praise: _____
10. How many chapters are in the book of Psalms? _____
11. David is known as _____.
12. Why was Psalm 51 written? _____
13. What is bloodguiltiness? _____
14. Name David's sacrifice to God: _____
15. What word is defined this way: "expressing or feeling sincere regret and remorse; remorseful" _____

Thank you for your participating in Dare Two Pray Bible study session. I hope you enjoyed this session.

Please send feedback to Daretwopray@gmail.com.
On a scale of 1 to 10 (1 being the least, 10 being the greatest), how was your experience with this lesson?

1 2 3 4 5 6 7 8 9 10

Leave Comments:
_____
_____

God Bless You!
In Love- Dare Two Pray

Talk Points/Knowledge Check Answer Key:

1. Who is one of the writers of the Books of Psalms? _____ David_____
2. Circle True or **False**: David wrote 75 of the 150 chapters of Psalms.
3. Fill in the blanks: The Lord is my __shepherd_ I shall _____not want__. Where is it found? __Psalm 23:1____
4. What is the name of the valley referred to in Psalm 23? ___Valley of the Shadow of Death_____
5. What is my head anointed with? __oil_____
6. How many instruments are used to praise God? _8 or (9 if you include your voice as an instrument)____
7. Where do you praise God? ___in the sanctuary and firmament (refers to the power that God has as He created the sky)
8. Circle True or **False**: David was the oldest son of Jesse.
9. Define Praise: _____ Merriam Webster -a sacred song or poem used in worship_____
10. How many chapters are in the book of Psalms? __150____
11. David is known as _____ A man after God's own heart_____.
12. Why was Psalm 51 written? ___ **Sinner's Prayer for Pardon. Repentance**_____
13. What is bloodguiltiness?_____Murder_____
14. Name David's sacrifice to God:___ "My [only] sacrifice [acceptable] to God is a broken spirit; A broken and contrite heart [broken with sorrow for sin, thoroughly penitent], such, O God, You will not despise" (Psalm 51:17).
15. What word is defined this way: "expressing or feeling sincere regret and remorse; remorseful" ____Repentant___

Lesson 1

- Knowing who David is shows the imperfection of a man of God. It shows how God will still find us favored, anointed, and use us, flaws and all.
- Although David was a sinner/imperfect man, he was chosen by God! When David sinned, he did what we all ought to do, repent and turn from his wicked ways.
- What does repentant mean? Repentant: expressing or feeling sincere regret and remorse; remorseful.
- When we sin, we displease God.
- How do you repent?
    - Pray to God, acknowledge your sin.
    - Tell the Lord you repent of your wrongdoings and will do them no more.
    - Pray against all the enemy's tactics and devices that will tempt you or cause you to fall; ask God to deliver you from evil.
    - Ask God for divine liberty, and affirm that you recommit yourself to His ways and will walk according to God's word.
    - Thank God for delivering you and forgiving you, and praise God as you walk

Lesson 2: What is a psalm? Merriam Webster: a sacred song or poem used in worship

Lesson 3: Psalm 23 was written by David during the time that his son rebelled against him, and he had to flee to Gilead. It is a psalm of strength/encouragement.

How many psalms did David write? He wrote 75; there are many other writers in the book of Psalms, and 48 of the authors remain unknown. https://www.gotquestions.org/Psalms-David.html

Definitions from OxfordDictionarys.com

Sanctuary: a sanctuary is a place that is holy or set apart for a holy purpose.

Firmament: the heavens or the sky, especially when regarded as a tangible thing:

Bloodguiltiness: murder.

Contrite: feeling or expressing remorse or penitence; affected by guilt:

Repentance: the action of repenting; sincere regret or remorse.

Timbrel: a tambourine or similar instrument.

Psaltery: an ancient stringed instrument similar to the lyre or zither but having a trapezoidal sounding board under the strings.

Hyssop (in biblical use): a wild shrub of uncertain identity whose twigs were used for sprinkling in ancient Jewish rites of purification.

Transgression: an act that goes against a law, rule, or code of conduct, an offense.

Righteousness: the quality of being morally right or justifiable.

About the Author

Minister Shenoa T. Gibson was born and raised in Maryland. At age eleven, in 1987, she received the gift of the Holy Ghost. She participated in several youth Choirs at the local church and within the Federation of Holy Trinity Churches. She served as the Youth and Adult Choir Director, drummer, and Sunday school and Vacation Bible School teacher. She served as the assistant church clerk for several years and on the deaconess board at the Northeast Holy Trinity Church, where they provided the foundation of spiritual necessities to ensure her growth in the Lord.

Minister Shenoa graduated from Laurel High School in 1994. She attended and completed college coursework at Prince George's Community College and Strayer College, with a concentration in business administration.

Her employment experience in the telecommunications industry was at Comcast and Verizon Wireless, which gave her more than 25 years of customer service and training and development experience. She currently works for a workforce development company. She has served the underprivileged population in Prince George's County, Maryland, by connecting them to community resources needed for basic life necessities and help in finding employment to become self-sufficient. She worked as a supervisor in partnership with the Department of Social Services. She has returned to what she most loved, teaching. She is a regional trainer in workforce development.

Being led by God in 2017, Minister Shenoa joined the Apostolic Breakthrough International Church under the leadership of Bishop Senyo Bullah. It was there she learned a deeper and intense level of connection to God in prayer and experienced the Holy Ghost fire in new ways. She served on the praise and worship team and played drums when needed. She was ordained as Minister in July 2018 by the Apostolic Breakthrough International Ministry.

Minister Shenoa prayed and was led by God to focus on developing and cultivating her own prayer line ministry, Dare Two Pray. The ministry started in July 2018, where God showed His power by connecting two coworkers together during a hardship, turning around a dire situation, creating a miraculous praise report, and showing what the *power of prayer* can do when two get together in Jesus's name! She was ordained by the Christian Global Outreach Ministries in 2019. The mission of Dare Two Pray is to synchronize with women and men in unwavering faith, in one accord, with one mind and boldness approaching the throne of the Almighty God in prayer. The Dare Two Pray scripture theme is Ecclesiastes 4:12: "A person standing alone can be attacked and defeated, but two can stand back-to-back and conquer. Three are even better, for a triple-braided cord is not easily broken." The ministry continues to grow with new callers, community work, and witnessing God move in miraculous ways.

Having obtained help from God, Minister Shenoa continues to this day witnessing to both great and small and will continue the work God has given her, striving for a crown of glory until her purpose has been fulfilled on this earth.

Made in the USA
Middletown, DE
30 July 2022